# CONTENTS

3A

# UNIT 1 How Are You?

## Mini Talk Look and listen. ▶ 🎧03

Good morning, Amy.

How are you?

Good morning.

I'm good. Thank you.

# Practice

**A** Listen and write the letter. 🎧 05    **B** Listen and repeat. 🎧 06

Good morning.    Good morning.

1 morning ☐

2 afternoon ☐

3 evening ☐

4 night ☐

How are you?    I'm great.

5 I'm great. ☐

6 I'm fine. ☐

7 Not bad. ☐

Not so good. ☐

8

# Listen & Talk

## A Listen and choose. 🎧07

1

2

3

4

5

6

## B Write and say.

How are you?

1

g_____

2

_____ so good

3

f_____

4

# Write & Talk

## A Listen, write, and read. 🎧08

| How | good | tired | great |
|-----|------|-------|-------|
| morning | | Not so good. | |

Good _____, Jane.

How are you?

I'm _____. How about you?

I'm _____. Thanks.

Hi, Eric. _____ are you?

_____

Are you _____?

Yes, I am.

## B Stick and write. Then ask and answer.

09:00 A.M.

Good morning.

How are you?

Sticker

07:00 P.M.

Good evening.

How _____?

Sticker

# Story

**Ⓐ Listen, write, and read.** ▶ 🎧09

| How | I'm | Great | for | Not so good. |

**B** Look and match.

How are you?

1  •

• ⓐ Not so good.

2  •

• ⓑ Great.

3  •

• ⓒ I'm fine.

**Draw faces. Then choose one and write.**

| I'm great. | I'm good. | Not bad. | Not so good. |

How are you?

_____ Thanks.

Song 10

# Check-Up

## A Listen and choose. 🎧11

1
  ⓐ
  ⓑ
  ⓒ

2
  ⓐ
  ⓑ
  ⓒ

## B Listen and match. 🎧12

## C Listen and choose. 🎧13

1  a  b  c
2  a  b  c
3  a  b  c
4  a  b  c

## D Read, check, and write.

**1**

Good _____, Mom.

☐ morning      ☐ night

**2**

A: How are you?

B: _____

☐ I'm good.      ☐ Not so good.

**3**

A: How are you?

B: _____ Thanks.

☐ I'm great.      ☐ Not bad.

## E Write and say.

**1**

Good evening.

**2**

I'm fine.

# Don't Touch, Please

## Mini Talk Look and listen. ▶ 🎧16

# Practice

**A** Listen and write the letter. 🎧18    **B** Listen and repeat. 🎧19

Don't talk, please.    Okay.

1. talk ☐

2. push ☐

3. enter ☐

4. run ☐

5. touch ☐

6. take pictures ☐

7. sit here ☐

8. eat here ☐

# Listen & Talk

**A** Listen and number. 🎧 20

**B** Write and say.

> Don't ... here, please.

1

_____

2

_____

3

_____

# Write & Talk

**A** **Listen, write, and read.** 🎧 21

| touch | pictures | Don't |
|---|---|---|
| sorry | please | |

🧑 I like this dress.

🧒 _____ _____, please.

🧑 Oh, I'm _____.

🧒 That's okay.

👧 Look at this!

🧑 Shh! Be quiet.

Don't take _____, _____.

🧒 Okay.

**B** **Look and write. Then say.**

eat here   talk   run   push

SCHOOL BUS RULES

1 Don't _____.

2 Don't _____.

3 _____

4 _____

# Story

## (A) Listen, write, and read. ▶ 🎧22

| touch | like | enter | nice | sit here |

## B Read and check.

1
Don't eat, please.
Don't enter, please.

2
Don't talk, please.
Don't touch, please.

3
Don't sit here, please.
Don't take pictures, please.

## Challenge

**Find the three people and circle. Then write.**

1 Don't _____.

2 Don't _____.

3 _____

**A** Listen and choose. 🎧24

1
   ⓐ
   ⓑ
   ⓒ

2
   ⓐ
   ⓑ
   ⓒ

**B** Listen and number. 🎧25

**C** Listen and choose. 🎧26

1
   ⓐ ⓑ

2
   ⓐ ⓑ

3
   ⓐ ⓑ

4
   ⓐ ⓑ

## D Read, check, and write.

**1**

A: Don't _____, please.
- ☐ enter
- ☐ sit here

B: Okay.

**2**

A: _____, please.
- ☐ Don't push
- ☐ Don't take pictures

B: Oh, I'm sorry.

**3**

A: _____, please.
- ☐ Don't run
- ☐ Don't touch

B: Oh, I'm sorry.

## E Write and say.

**1**

Oh, I'm sorry.

**2**

Okay.

# Review 1

**A** Choose and write.

| night | morning | afternoon |
|---|---|---|

1 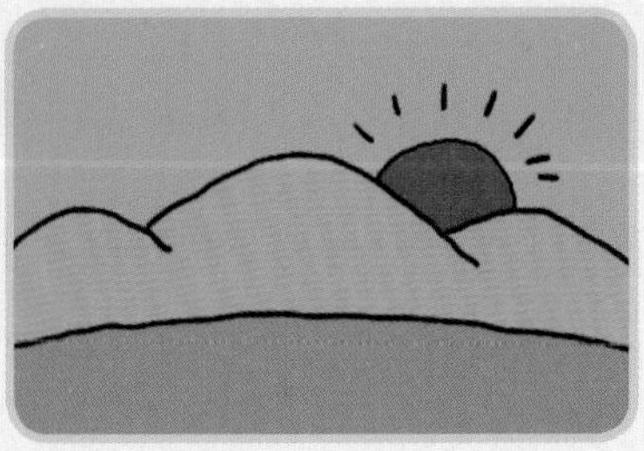

____________

2 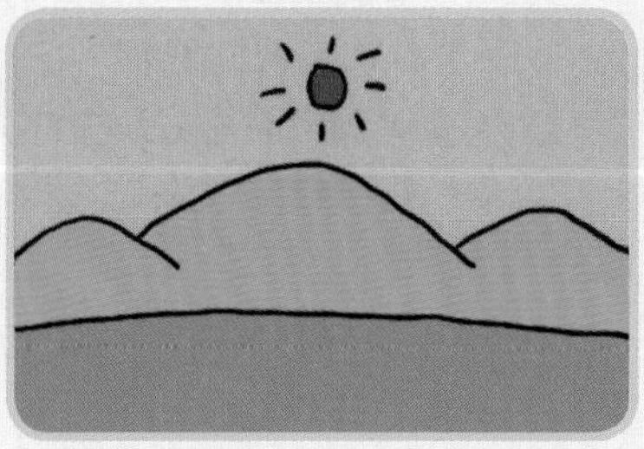

____________

3 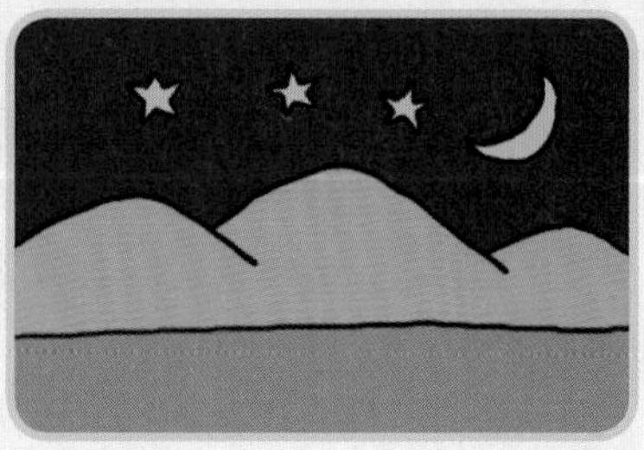

____________

| not bad | great | not so good |
|---|---|---|

4 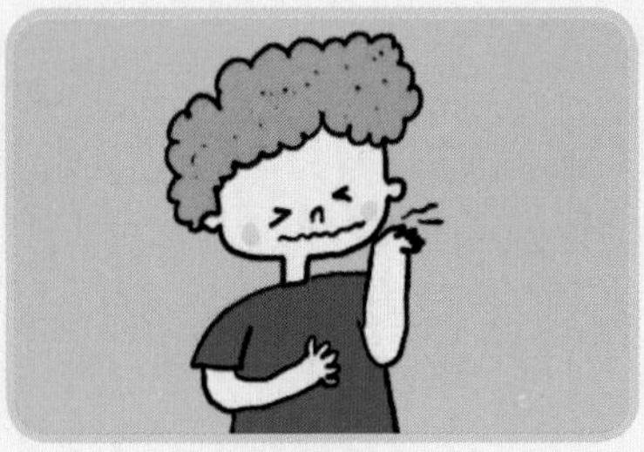

____________

5 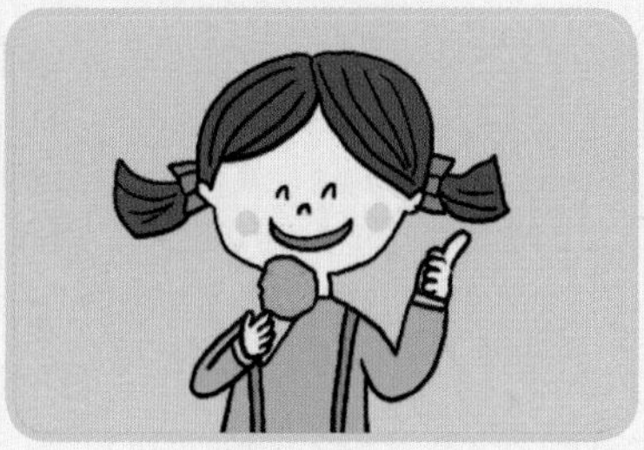

____________

6 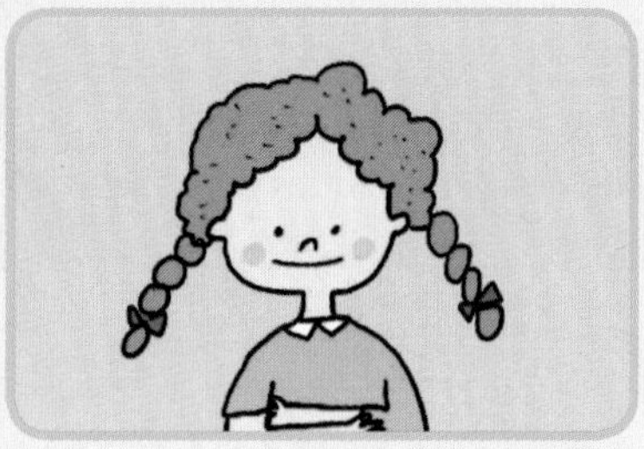

____________

| run | push | take pictures |
|---|---|---|

7 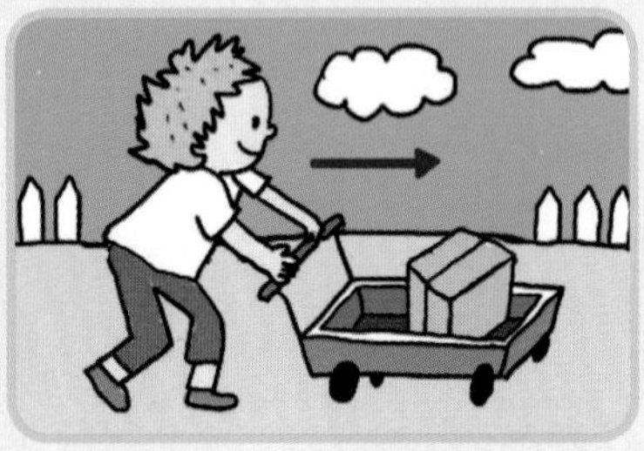

____________

8 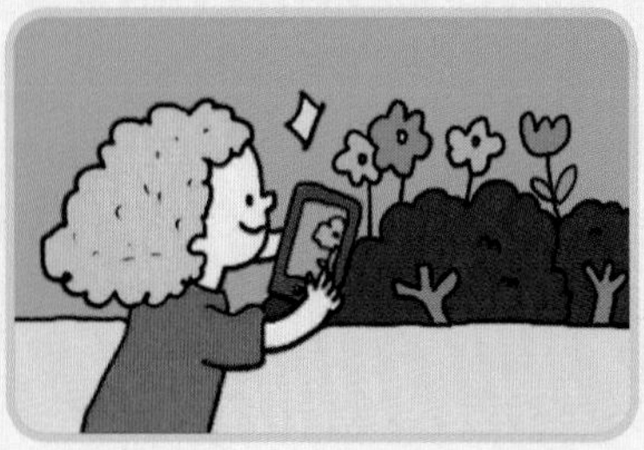

____________

9 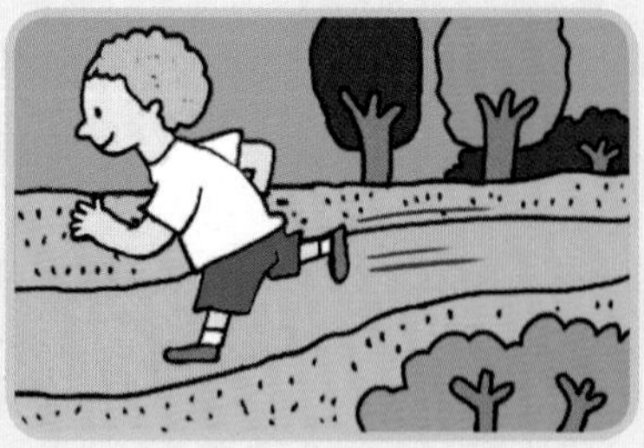

____________

**B** **Read and number.**

1 Don't touch, please.

2 Don't enter, please.

3 Don't sit here, please.

4 Don't eat here, please.

**C** **Read, choose, and write.**

A: Good morning.

B: _____

A: How are you?

B: _____

A: Good evening.

B: _____

A: How are you?

B: _____

| Good evening. | Good morning. | I'm fine. | Not so good. |

# What Time Is It?

## Mini Talk Look and listen. ▶ 🎧29

What time is it?

It's nine o'clock.

Oh, I'm late.

Today is Saturday.

# Practice

What time is it?    It's one o'clock.

1 one o'clock ☐

2 one ten ☐

3 four fifteen ☐

4 five twenty ☐

5 eight thirty ☐

6 eleven forty ☐

7 twelve fifty ☐

# Listen & Talk

## Ⓐ Listen, write, and match. 🎧33

1 [ _ : _ ] •

2 [ _ : _ ] •

3 [ _ : _ ] •

4 [ _ : _ ] •

5 [ _ : _ ] •

ⓐ
ⓑ
ⓒ
ⓓ
ⓔ

## Ⓑ Write and say.

What time is it?

1  12:50

2  03:15

3  08:10

twelve _____     three _____     eight _____

# Write & Talk

## A Listen, write, and read. 34

| thirty | seven | time |
|--------|-------|------|
| morning | late | it |

Good _____, Emma.

Good morning, Dad.

What _____ is it?

It's _____ o'clock.

What time is _____?

It's eight _____.

We're _____. Let's go.

## B Check and write. Then ask and answer.

What time is it?

1

☐ eight forty
☐ eight fifty

It's _____.

2

☐ six ten
☐ six thirty

It's _____.

3

☐ eleven o'clock
☐ twelve o'clock

It's _____.

# Story

**A** Listen, write, and read. ▶ 🎧35

time     o'clock     thirty     two     not

24

## B Read and match.

What time is it?

1 It's two o'clock.    2 It's two thirty.    3 It's three o'clock.

## Challenge

**Draw the time and write.**

① It's _____.

② It's _____.

36 Song

**A** Listen and choose. 🎧37

1

a

b

c

2

a

b

c

**B** Listen and match. 🎧38

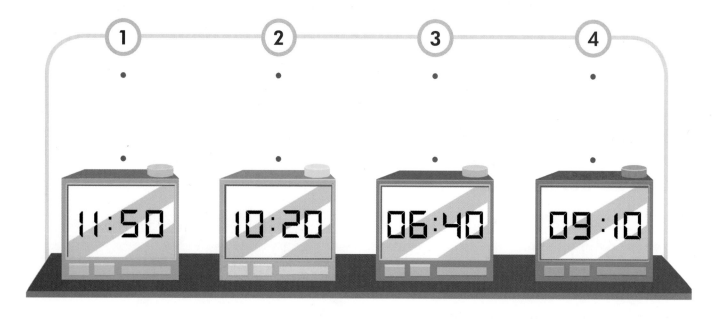

**C** Listen and draw. 🎧39

1  2  3 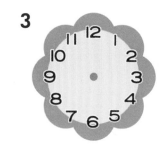 4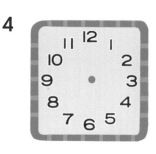

## D Look and write.

What time is it?

**1**

It's _____ thirty.

**2**

It's _____ _____.

**3**

It's _____ _____.

## E Write and say.

**1**

What time is it?

**2**

What time is it?

# Let's Play Badminton

## Mini Talk Look and listen. ▶ 42

Let's play badminton.

Sounds good.

Two days later

Let's play basketball.

Sorry, I can't. I'm busy.

SCHOOL

43 CHECK 1 a ☐ b ☐  2 a ☐ b ☐

# Practice

**A** Listen and write the letter. 🎧 44    **B** Listen and repeat. 🎧 45

Let's play soccer.

Sounds good.

Sorry, I can't.

1 play soccer ☐ 🙂

2 play basketball ☐ 🙁

3 play baseball ☐ 🙂

4 fly a kite ☐ 🙂

5 make a snowman ☐ 🙁

6 play badminton ☐ 🙂

7 ride a bike ☐ 🙁

# Listen & Talk

## (A) Listen, match, and circle. 🎧46

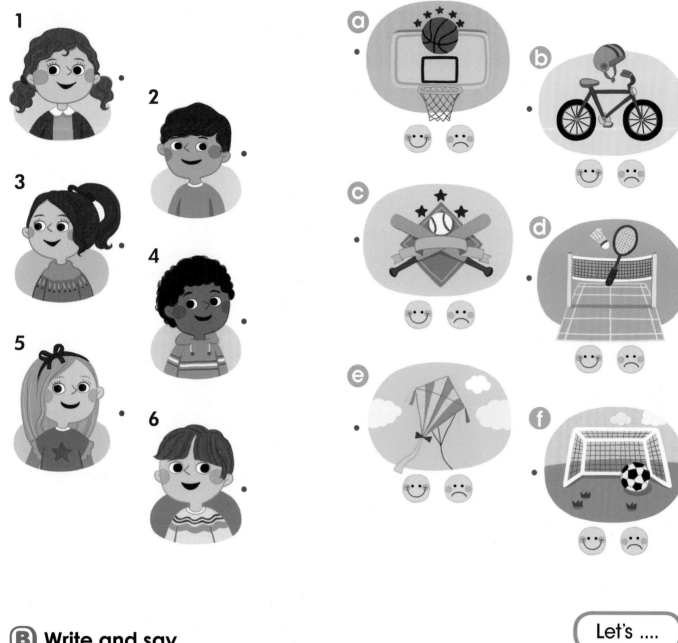

**1**

**2**

**3**

**4**

**5**

**6**

a

b

c

d

e

f

## (B) Write and say.

Let's ....

**1** _____ a kite

**2** _____ baseball

**3** _____ a snowman

# Write & Talk

## A Listen, write, and read. 🎧 47

| ride | can't | Okay. |
|------|-------|-------|
| Let's | tired | snowman |

👦 Can you _____ a bike?

👧 Yes, I can.

👦 _____ ride a bike.

👧 _____

👧 It's snowing.

Let's make a _____.

👦 Sorry, I _____. I'm _____.

👧 That's okay.

## B Stick and write. Then say.

| soccer | basketball |
|--------|------------|
| Sounds good. | Sorry, I can't. |

A: Let's play _____.

B: _____

A: Let's play _____.

B: _____

# Story

## Ⓐ Listen, write, and read. ▶ 🎧48

1

Don't touch it.

Okay.

2

Let's _____.

Sorry, I can't. I'm _____.

3

Let's _____.

Sorry, I can't. I'm busy.

4

Let's make a cake.

_____

5

6

I'm not _____. Yummy!

| ride a bike | play badminton | tired | busy | Sounds good. |

## B Read and number in order. Then check.

◯ Let's make a cake.

☐ Sounds good.
☐ Sorry, I can't.

◯ Let's ride a bike.

☐ Sounds good.
☐ Sorry, I can't.

◯ Let's play badminton.

☐ Sounds good.
☐ Sorry, I can't.

## Challenge

**Choose and write.**

A: Let's play basketball.

B: Sounds good.

A: Let's _____.

B: _____

# Check-Up

## A Listen and choose. 🎧 50

1   ⓐ ⓑ ⓒ

2   ⓐ ⓑ ⓒ

## B Listen and write T or F. 🎧 51

1

2

3

4

## C Listen, number, and match. 🎧 52

Sounds good.

Sorry, I can't.

## D Read, write, and check.

**1**

A: Let's _____ _____.

B: ☐ Sounds good. ☐ Sorry, I can't.

**2**

A: Let's _____ _____.

B: ☐ Sounds good. ☐ Sorry, I can't.

**3**

A: Let's _____ a _____.

B: ☐ Sounds good. ☐ Sorry, I can't.

## E Write and say.

**1** Let's make a snowman.

**2** Sorry, I can't. I'm tired.

**A** Choose and write.

**1**  `11:00`
- fly a _____
- ___eleven___ o'clock

**2**  `12:00`
- play _____
- _____ o'clock

**3**  `01:15`
- _____ a bike
- one _____

**4**  `03:20`
- _____ badminton
- three _____

**5**  `04:50`
- play _____
- four _____

| play | ride | soccer | basketball | kite |
|------|------|--------|------------|------|
| eleven | twelve | fifteen | twenty | fifty |

**Ⓑ Read and number.**

What time is it?

**1**   It's ten o'clock.

**2**   It's six ten.

**3**   It's twelve forty.

**4**   It's eleven thirty.

**Ⓒ Follow, write, and check.**

**1**

A: Let's _____.
B: ☐ Sounds good.
   ☐ Sorry, I can't.

**2**

A: Let's _____.
B: ☐ Sounds good.
   ☐ Sorry, I can't.

**3**

A: Let's _____.
B: ☐ Sounds good.
   ☐ Sorry, I can't.

ride a bike          make a snowman          play baseball

# Is This Your Watch?

**Mini Talk** Look and listen. ▶ 🎧55

Is that your watch?

No, it isn't.
My watch is yellow.

Is this your watch?

Yes, it is.
Thank you.

56
CHECK  1 a ☐ b ☐  2 a ☐ b ☐

# Practice

**A** Listen and write the letter.  57

**B** Listen and repeat.  58

Is this your cap / hairpin?

1 cap
2 towel
3 belt
4 watch

5 hairpin
6 camera
7 backpack
8 umbrella

Yes, it is.

No, it isn't.
My hairpin is green.

# Listen & Talk

**Ⓐ Listen and circle.** 🎧59

1  ⓐ  ⓑ

2  ⓐ  ⓑ

3  ⓐ  ⓑ

4  ⓐ  ⓑ

5  ⓐ  ⓑ

6  ⓐ  ⓑ

**Ⓑ Write and say.**

Is this your ...?

1  Yes

2  No

3  Yes

t_____

u_____

c_____

# Write & Talk

**A** Listen, write, and read. 🎧 60

| is | big | your |
|----|-----|------|
| my | that | umbrella |

Is this _____ hairpin?

No, it isn't. My hairpin is _____.

Oh, it's _____ hairpin.

Thank you.

Where is my _____?

Is _____ your umbrella?

Yes, it _____. Thank you.

**B** Look and write. Then ask and answer.

| watch |
|-------|
| backpack |
| cap |

1  A: Is this your _____?    B: _____, it _____.

2  A: Is this your _____?    B: _____, it _____.

3  A: Is this your _____?    B: _____, it _____.

# Story

A Picnic Day

Ⓐ Listen, write, and read. ▶ 🎧61

Let's   backpack   camera   My   cap   yellow

42

## B Read and match.

1  Is this your camera?  •

 • Yes, it is.

2  Is that your backpack?  •

 • No, it isn't.

3  Is this your cap?  •

 • Yes, it is.

 • No, it isn't.

## Challenge

**Mark O or X. Choose and write.**

1 A: Is this your _____?

  B: _____, _____.

2 A: Is this your _____?

  B: _____, _____.

# Check-Up

## A Listen and choose. 🎧63

1  (a) (b) (c)

2  (a) (b) (c)

## B Listen and choose. 🎧64

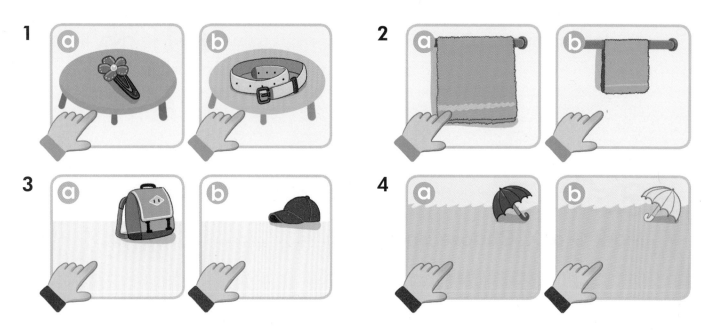

1  (a) (b)

2  (a) (b)

3  (a) (b)

4  (a) (b)

## C Listen, choose, and write the letter. 🎧65

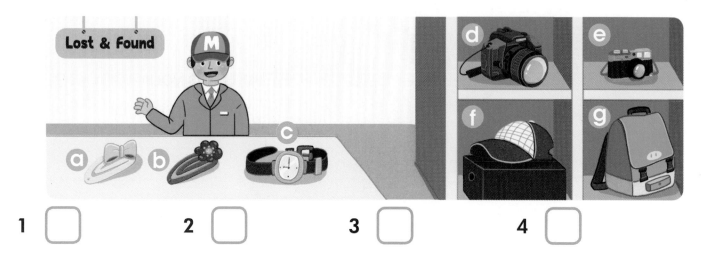

Lost & Found

1 ☐  2 ☐  3 ☐  4 ☐

## D Read, check, and write.

**1**

A: Is this _____?

☐ your belt  ☐ your watch

B: Yes, it is.

**2**

A: Is that your cap?

B: _____ My cap is red.

☐ Yes, it is.  ☐ No, it isn't.

**3**

A: Is this your umbrella?

B: _____

☐ Yes, it is.  ☐ No, it isn't.

## E Write and say.

**1**

Yes, it is.

**2**

Is that your backpack?

_____
My backpack is _____.

# It's On the Table

## Mini Talk Look and listen. ▶ 🎧 68

## CHECK 69  1 a ☐  b ☐   2 a ☐  b ☐

# Practice

**A** Listen and write the letter. 🎧70  **B** Listen and repeat. 🎧71

Where is my T-shirt? | It's on the bed.

1 T-shirt — on the bed ☐

2 cap — on the table ☐

3 bat — under the table ☐

4 ball — in the box ☐

5 watch — on the desk ☐

6 glove — under the chair ☐

7 book — in the bag ☐

# Listen & Talk

**Ⓐ Listen and stick.** 🎧72

**Ⓑ Write and say.**

> It's / They're ....

1

_____ the table

2

_____ the chair

3

_____ the box

48

# Write & Talk

## A Listen, write, and read. 🎧73

| chair | scissors | cap |
|-------|----------|-----|
| not | under | in |

🗣️ Where is my _____?

🙂 It's on the desk.

🗣️ No, it's _____ here.

🙂 Oh, it's _____ the box.

🗣️ Where are my _____?

🙂 I don't know.

🗣️ Look! They're _____ the _____.

🙂 Thank you.

## B Match and write. Then ask and answer.

| table | bag | bed |
|-------|-----|-----|

1

2

3

ⓐ Where is my bat?

It's _____.

ⓑ Where are my crayons?

They're _____.

ⓒ Where are my sunglasses?

They're _____.

# Story

**Ⓐ Listen, write, and read.** ▶ 🎧74

1. Where is my _____?
   It's _____ the bed.

2. Where is my _____?
   It's _____ the box.

3. Where are my _____?
   They're _____ the tree.

4. Oh, it's twelve.
   Yeah!

5. Let's go!
   Okay.

| bags | on | belt | hat | under | in |

## B Read, circle, and check.

**1**

A: Where is the ( watch / belt )?

B: ☐ It's on the table.　　☐ It's on the bed.

**2**

A: Where is the ( hat / T-shirt )?

B: ☐ It's in the box.　　☐ It's on the box.

**3**

A: Where are the ( bags / boots )?

B: ☐ They're under the tree.　☐ They're on the desk.

## Challenge

**Find the two differences. Then write.**

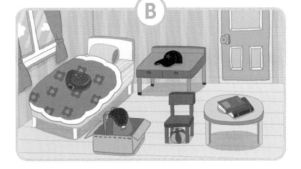

**1** Where is the _____?

Ⓐ It's _____.

Ⓑ It's _____.

**2** Where are the _____?

Ⓐ They're _____.

Ⓑ They're _____.

75 Song

# Check-Up

## A Listen and number. 🎧76

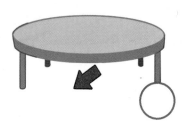 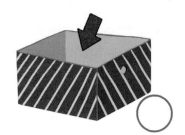 

## B Listen and choose. 🎧77

1
ⓐ ⓑ

2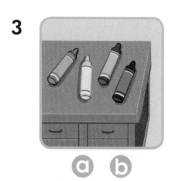
ⓐ ⓑ

3
ⓐ ⓑ

4
ⓐ ⓑ

## C Listen and circle. 🎧78

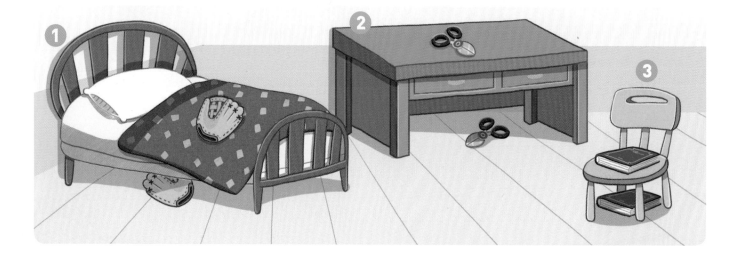

# D Read, check, and write.

1

**A:** Where is my camera?

**B:** It's _____.

☐ on the chair    ☐ under the chair

2

**A:** Where are my balls?

**B:** They're _____.

☐ on the bed    ☐ under the desk

3

**A:** Where is my cap?

**B:** It's _____.

☐ in the box    ☐ on the table

# E Write and say.

1

Where is my watch?

2

They're in the bag.

# Review 3

**Ⓐ Circle and write.**

| | | |
|---|---|---|
| 1 | ( on / under ) the desk | b ____ ____ t |
| 2 | ( under / on ) the bed | b a ____ k p a ____ k |
| 3 | ( under / on ) the chair | w a t ____ h |
| 4 | ( under / on ) the table | u ____ b r e l ____ a |
| 5 | ( on / in ) the box | ____ a m e ____ a |

## Ⓑ Read and number.

**1**

A: Is this your camera?

B: Yes, it is.

**2**

A: Is this your umbrella?

B: No, it isn't.
My umbrella is yellow.

**3**

A: Is this your backpack?

B: No, it isn't.
My backpack is green.

## Ⓒ Read, choose, and write.

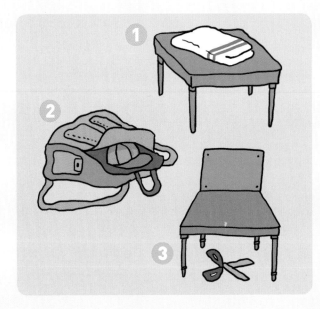

**1**

A: Where is my _____?

B: It's _____ the table.

**2**

A: Where is my _____?

B: It's _____ the bag.

**3**

A: Where are my _____?

B: They're _____ the chair.

| in | scissors | on | towel | cap | under |

# I Want a Hairpin

## Mini Talk Look and listen. ▶ 🎧81

I'm Genie.
Do you want some shoes?

No, I don't.

What do you want?

I want a hairpin.

🎧82 CHECK 1 a ☐ b ☐ 2 a ☐ b ☐

# Practice

**A** Listen and write the letter. 🎧83    **B** Listen and repeat. 🎧84

Flea Market

What do you want?

I want a scarf.

1 a scarf ☐

2 a kite ☐

3 a puzzle ☐

4 a jump rope ☐

5 a comic book ☐
COMIC 1

6 mittens ☐

7 socks ☐

8 shoes ☐

# Listen & Talk

## A Listen and stick. 🎧 85

## B Write and say.

I want ....

1. I

a s_____

2. We

a k_____

3. They

s_____

58

# Write & Talk

**Ⓐ Listen, write, and read.** 🎧 86

| hat | What | Do |
|-----|------|-----|
| want | ring | you |

👦 _____ do you _____ ?

🧒 I want a _____ .

👦 Here you are.

🧒 Thank you.

👦 _____ you want a hat, too?

👧 No, I don't.

👦 What do _____ want?

👧 I want a _____ .

**Ⓑ Look and write. Then ask and answer.**

I want ....

I don't want ....

1  A: Do you want a watch?

   B: _____ , I _____ .

.........................................................

2  A: Do you want a pencil case?

   B: _____ , I _____ .

.........................................................

3  A: Do you want socks?

   B: _____ , _____ _____ .

# Story

**A** Listen, write, and read. ▶ 🎧 87

1. What do you want?
   I want a _____.

2. How about you?
   I _____ a puzzle.

3. Do you want a _____?
   Yes, I do.

4. _____ do you want?
   I want socks.

5. Hello!
   They're cute.
   We want _____, too.

| want | What | kite | socks | basketball |

**B** **Read and match.**

What do you want?

1  • • **a** I want a kite. • •

2  • • **b** I want a basketball. • •

3  • • **c** I want socks. • •

**Choose three things and write.**

MERRY CHRISTMAS

I want a _____.

I _____.

I _____.

Merry Christmas, Santa!

# Check-Up

## A Listen and write the letter. 🎧89

1    2    3

## B Listen and choose. 🎧90

1 ⓐ ⓑ      2 ⓐ ⓑ

3 ⓐ ⓑ      4 ⓐ ⓑ

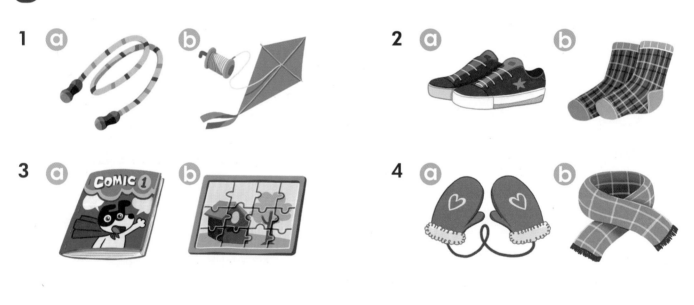

## C Listen and choose. 🎧91

1    2    3

ⓐ ⓑ      ⓐ ⓑ      ⓐ ⓑ

## D Read, check, and write.

**1**

A: What do you want?

B: I want _____.

☐ a jump rope   ☐ shoes

**2**

A: Do you want mittens?

B: _____

☐ Yes, I do.   ☐ No, I don't.

**3**

A: What do you want?

B: We want _____.

☐ a puzzle   ☐ a kite

## E Write and say.

**1**

What do you want?

**2**

Do you want a scarf?

# Do You Want Some Soup?

**Mini Talk** Look and listen.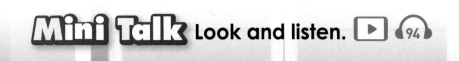

Do you want some soup?

Yes, please. It's good.

No, thanks. I'm full.

CHECK    1  a ☐  b ☐    2  a ☐  b ☐

64

# Practice

**A** Listen and write the letter. 🎧96  **B** Listen and repeat. 🎧97

Do you want some soup?

Yes, please.

No, thanks.

1. soup ☐
2. water ☐
3. yogurt ☐
4. cheesecake ☐
5. apple pie ☐
6. ice cream ☐
7. cookies ☐
8. strawberries ☐

# Listen & Talk

**Ⓐ Listen, match, and mark O or X.** 🎧 98

1   2   3   4   5   6

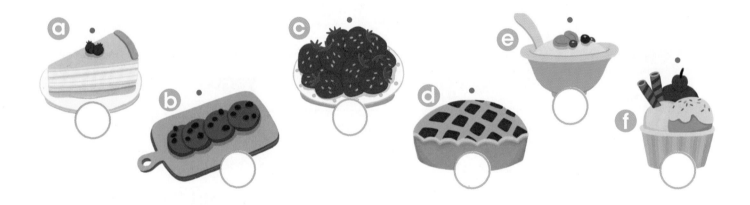

ⓐ   ⓑ   ⓒ   ⓓ   ⓔ   ⓕ

**Ⓑ Write and say.**

I want some ....

1   I

w_____

2   We

s_____

3   They

a_____

# Write & Talk

## A Listen, write, and read. 🎧99

strawberries    some    ice cream
No, thanks.    Yes, please.

🧑 Do you want _____ yogurt?

👧 _____

🧑 What do you want?

👧 I want some _____.

🧑 Do you want some _____?

👧 _____

🧑 Help yourself.

👧 Thanks. It's delicious!

## B Write and check. Then ask and answer.

soup    cookies
cheesecake

MENU

1  Do you want some _____?
   ☐ Yes, please.    ☐ No, thanks.

2  Do you want _____ _____?
   ☐ Yes, please.    ☐ No, thanks.

3  Do you want _____ _____?
   ☐ Yes, please.    ☐ No, thanks.

# Story

**Ⓐ Listen, write, and read.** ▶ 🎧100

1. Do you want some cheesecake?

2. Do you want some cheesecake, too?

3. I _____ some strawberries.

4. What do you want?

   I want _____ carrot soup.

5. Help yourself!

   Thank you.

   I _____ strawberries.

   It's delicious.

| like | Yes, please. | want | some | No, thanks. |

## B Read and match.

What do you want?

1  I want •

2  I want •

3  I want •

a • some strawberries.

b • some carrot soup.

c • some cheesecake.

## Challenge

Choose, draw, and write.

A: Do you want some _____?

B: _____, _____.

A: Do you want some _____?

B: _____, _____.

# Check-Up

**A** Listen and choose. 🎧102

1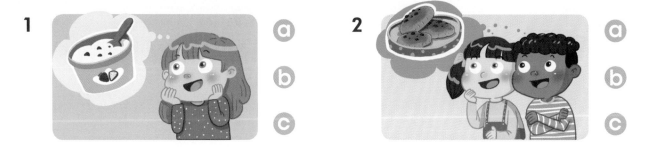
ⓐ
ⓑ
ⓒ

2
ⓐ
ⓑ
ⓒ

**B** Listen and number. Then choose Yes or No. 🎧103

Yes No    Yes No    Yes No    Yes No

**C** Listen and choose. 🎧104

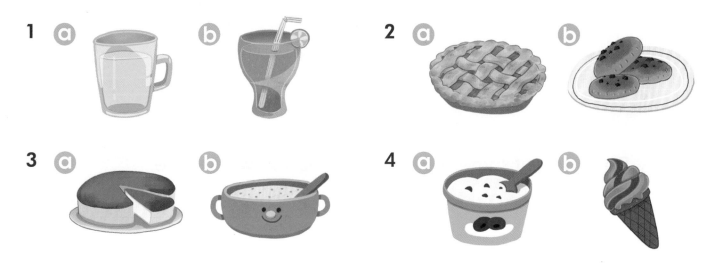

1 ⓐ  ⓑ    2 ⓐ  ⓑ

3 ⓐ  ⓑ    4 ⓐ  ⓑ

70

## D Read, check, and write.

**1**

A: Do you want _____?

☐ some yogurt ☐ some cookies

B: Yes, please.

**2**

A: What do you want?

B: I want _____.

☐ some juice ☐ some ice cream

**3**

A: Do you want some apple pie?

B: _____ I'm full.

☐ Yes, please. ☐ No, thanks.

## E Write and say.

**1**

Yes, please.

**2**

No, thanks.

# Review 4

**A** Look and match.

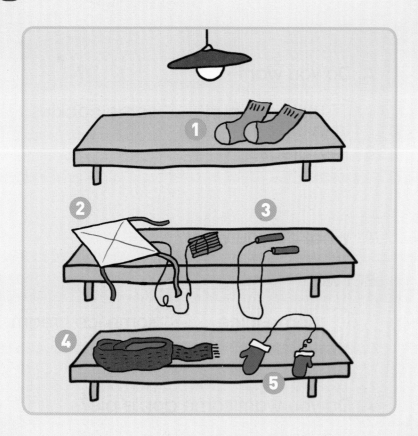

- socks
- a jump rope
- a scarf
- mittens
- a kite

- cheesecake
- yogurt
- apple pie
- strawberries
- cookies

**B** Read and number.

What do you want?

○ I want a puzzle.

○ I want a comic book.

○ I want shoes.

○ I want mittens.

**C** Look and write. Then check.

1
A: Do you want some _____?
B: ○ Yes, please. ○ No, thanks.

2
A: Do you want some _____?
B: ○ Yes, please. ○ No, thanks.

3
A: Do you want some _____?
B: ○ Yes, please. ○ No, thanks.

4
A: Do you want some _____?
B: ○ Yes, please. ○ No, thanks.

water          ice cream          cookies          soup

# Songs

## Unit 1 How Are You?

Good morning. How are you?

I'm great. Thanks.

Good afternoon. How are you?

I'm fine. Thanks.

Good evening. How are you?

Not bad. Thanks.

## Unit 2 Don't Run 🎧23

Don't run. Don't run.

Okay. Okay.

Don't push. Don't push.

Oh, I'm sorry.

Don't touch. Don't touch.

Okay. Okay.

Don't enter. Don't enter.

Oh, I'm sorry.

## Unit 3 What Time Is It?

Tick-tock, tick-tock. What time is it?

It's six. It's six o'clock.

Tick-tock, tick-tock. What time is it?

It's eight thirty. Good morning!

Tick-tock, tick-tock. What time is it?

It's eleven forty. Good night!

## Unit 4 Let's Ride a Bike 🎧49

Let's ride a bike.

Let's fly a kite.

Sounds good. Good.

Let's play basketball.

Let's make a snowman.

Sorry, I can't. Sorry.

## Unit 5 Is This Your Watch? 🎧62

Is this your watch?

   Yes, it is. Here it is.

Is this your umbrella?

   No, it isn't. My umbrella is blue.

Is this your cap?

   Yes, it is. Here it is.

Is this your backpack?

   No, it isn't. My backpack is yellow.

## Unit 6 It's In the Box 🎧75

(Hmm) Where is my cap?

   It's in the box.

(Hmm) Where is my watch?

   It's on the table.

(Hmm) Where are my books?

   They're under the bed.

   Here you are.

Thank you.

## Unit 7 I Want a Scarf 🎧88

What do you want?

What do you want?

   I want a scarf.

   I want a belt.

What do you want?

What do you want?

   I want socks.

   I want shoes.

## Unit 8 Do You Want Some Water? 🎧101

Do you want some water?

   Yes, please. Thank you.

Do you want some cookies?

   No, thanks. I'm full.

Do you want some yogurt?

   Yes, please. Thank you.

Do you want some strawberries?

   No, thanks. I'm full.

## Ⓐ Listen, circle, and match. 🎧105

| 1 | | 2 | | 3 | | 4 | |
|---|---|---|---|---|---|---|---|
| bike | | name | | cube | | note | |
| tube | | nose | | kite | | make | |

## Ⓑ Listen and circle. 🎧106

| 1 | make | bike | nose | 2 | flute | home | tape |
|---|---|---|---|---|---|---|---|
| 3 | kite | cute | cake | 4 | dive | cube | note |

## Ⓒ Circle and write.

1

| ike | ake |
|---|---|

b_____

2

| ose | ube |
|---|---|

c_____

3

| ake | ite |
|---|---|

m_____

# Phonics 2

## A Listen and repeat. Then read. 🎧107

ai
ay

1 ai ➡ rain

2 ai ➡ tail

3 ai ➡ wait

4 ay ➡ say

5 ay ➡ May

6 ay ➡ day

## B Listen and circle. 🎧108

1 tape
tail

2 day
rain

3 say
May

4 way
walt

## C Circle and write.

1  M  N  a  y  _____

2  r  e  a  i  n  _____

3  s  a  i  y  _____

## Ⓐ Listen and repeat. Then read. 🎧109

ee
ea
ey

1 ee → see

2 ee → feet

3 ea → eat

4 ea → clean

5 ey → monkey

6 ey → honey

## Ⓑ Listen and check. 🎧110

1 ☐ feet ☐ eat

2 ☐ read ☐ see

3 ☐ monkey ☐ honey

4 ☐ eat ☐ meet

## Ⓒ Match and write.

1

2

3

f___ ___t

___ ___t

monk___ ___

# Phonics ④

 Phonics ④   Review: ai, ay, ee, ea, ey

## Ⓐ Listen, circle, and write. 🎧111

| 1 | ee  ay  ey | 2 | ee  ay  ai | 3 | ay  ey  ea | 4 | ee  ai  ea |

1  f___ ___t

2  d___ ___

3  hon___ ___

4  t___ ___l

## Ⓑ Listen, circle, and match. 🎧112

| 1 | rain | 2 | monkey | 3 | feet | 4 | say |
|   | feet |   | May    |   | eat  |   | see |

## Ⓒ Circle and write.

1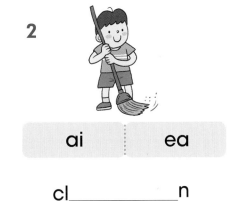

| ay | ey |

s_____

2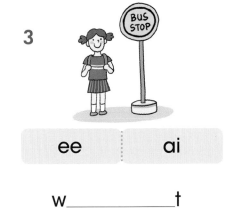

| ai | ea |

cl_____n

3

| ee | ai |

w_____t

**A** Listen and repeat. Then read. 🎧113

| | | |
|---|---|---|
| **ie** **igh** | 1 ie → pie  | 4 igh → night  |
| | 2 ie → tie  | 5 igh → fight  |
| | 3 ie → lie  | 6 igh → bright  |

**B** Listen and check. 🎧114

1
☐ pie
☐ fight

2
☐ lie
☐ night

3
☐ tie
☐ bright

**C** Circle and write.

1

ie   igh ○— p_____

2

ie   igh ○— n_____t

3

ie   igh ○— f_____t

## Ⓐ Listen and repeat. Then read. 🎧115

**oa**
**ow**

1 oa → coat

2 oa → goat

3 oa → soap

4 ow → snow

5 ow → blow

6 ow → bowl

## Ⓑ Listen and circle. 🎧116

1  boat  coat  snow

2  goat  bowl  blow

3  goat  road  soap

4  coat  soap  snow

## Ⓒ Match and write.

1   •  •  b___ ___l

2   •  •  s___ ___p

3   •  •  c___ ___t

## Ⓐ Listen and repeat. Then read.

# ue
# ui

1 ue → blue

2 ue → glue

3 ue → clue

4 ui → juice

5 ui → suit

6 ui → fruit

## Ⓑ Listen and circle. 118

1    blue    suit    true        2    clue    true    fruit

3    true    suit    juice       4    suit    blue    glue

## Ⓒ Circle and write.

1

| ue | ui |

fr_____t

2

| ue | ui |

gl_____

3

| ue | ui |

s_____t

**(A) Listen, circle, and write.** 🎧119

| 1 | ue igh oa | 2 | oa ie ui | 3 | igh ow ie | 4 | ui ie ow |
|---|-----------|---|----------|---|-----------|---|----------|
| | br_____t | | c_____t | | p_____ | | fr_____t |

**(B) Listen, circle, and match.** 🎧120

| 1 | tie | 2 | snow | 3 | fight | 4 | bright |
|---|-----|---|------|---|-------|---|--------|
| | glue | | soap | | fruit | | blue |

**(C) Look and check.**

1

☐ lie
☐ night

2

☐ bowl
☐ soap

3

☐ clue
☐ juice

# Word List

## Unit 1 How Are You?

afternoon _____

evening _____

fine _____

good _____

great _____

how _____

morning _____

night _____

not bad _____

not so good _____

tired _____

## Unit 2 Don't Touch, Please

eat here _____

enter _____

look at _____

okay _____

please _____

push _____

quiet _____

run _____

sit here _____

sorry _____

take pictures _____

talk _____

touch _____

## Unit 3 What Time Is It?

eleven _____

fifteen _____

fifty _____

forty _____

go _____

late _____

o'clock _____

ten _____

thirty _____

time _____

twelve _____

twenty _____

we _____

## Unit 4 Let's Play Badminton

busy _____

can _____

fly a kite _____

let's _____

make a snowman _____

play badminton _____

play baseball _____

play basketball _____

play soccer _____

ride a bike _____

snowing _____

## Unit 5　Is This Your Watch?

backpack　　＿＿＿＿＿＿＿

belt　　　　＿＿＿＿＿＿＿

big　　　　＿＿＿＿＿＿＿

camera　　＿＿＿＿＿＿＿

cap　　　　＿＿＿＿＿＿＿

hairpin　　＿＿＿＿＿＿＿

my　　　　＿＿＿＿＿＿＿

small　　　＿＿＿＿＿＿＿

towel　　　＿＿＿＿＿＿＿

umbrella　＿＿＿＿＿＿＿

watch　　　＿＿＿＿＿＿＿

your　　　　＿＿＿＿＿＿＿

## Unit 6　It's On the Table

glove　　　　　　＿＿＿＿＿＿＿

in the bag　　　＿＿＿＿＿＿＿

in the box　　　＿＿＿＿＿＿＿

know　　　　　　＿＿＿＿＿＿＿

on the bed　　　＿＿＿＿＿＿＿

on the desk　　＿＿＿＿＿＿＿

on the table　　＿＿＿＿＿＿＿

scissors　　　　＿＿＿＿＿＿＿

shorts　　　　　＿＿＿＿＿＿＿

sunglasses　　＿＿＿＿＿＿＿

under the chair　＿＿＿＿＿＿＿

under the table　＿＿＿＿＿＿＿

where　　　　　＿＿＿＿＿＿＿

## Unit 7　I Want a Hairpin

comic book　　＿＿＿＿＿＿＿

here　　　　　＿＿＿＿＿＿＿

jump rope　　＿＿＿＿＿＿＿

kite　　　　　＿＿＿＿＿＿＿

mittens　　　＿＿＿＿＿＿＿

pencil case　＿＿＿＿＿＿＿

puzzle　　　　＿＿＿＿＿＿＿

ring　　　　　＿＿＿＿＿＿＿

scarf　　　　＿＿＿＿＿＿＿

shoes　　　　＿＿＿＿＿＿＿

socks　　　　＿＿＿＿＿＿＿

want　　　　＿＿＿＿＿＿＿

## Unit 8　Do You Want Some Soup?

apple pie　　　＿＿＿＿＿＿＿

cheesecake　＿＿＿＿＿＿＿

cookies　　　＿＿＿＿＿＿＿

delicious　　　＿＿＿＿＿＿＿

full　　　　　＿＿＿＿＿＿＿

hungry　　　　＿＿＿＿＿＿＿

ice cream　　＿＿＿＿＿＿＿

some　　　　＿＿＿＿＿＿＿

soup　　　　＿＿＿＿＿＿＿

strawberries　＿＿＿＿＿＿＿

water　　　　＿＿＿＿＿＿＿

yogurt　　　　＿＿＿＿＿＿＿

# Syllabus 3A

## Unit 1  How Are You?

| Structures | Vocabulary | | Phonics |
|---|---|---|---|
| • Good morning. | morning | fine | Review: Long Vowels |
|   Good morning. | afternoon | not bad | a-e, i-e, o-e, u-e |
| • How are you? | evening | not so good | |
|   I'm great. Thanks. | night | sick | |
| • I'm sick. | great | tired | |

## Unit 2  Don't Touch, Please

| Structures | Vocabulary | | Phonics |
|---|---|---|---|
| • Don't talk, please. | talk | take pictures | Long Vowels |
|   Okay. | push | sit here | ai, ay |
| • Oh, I'm sorry. | enter | eat here | |
|   That's okay. | run | please | |
| • Look at that. / Be quiet. | touch | | |

**Review 1**

## Unit 3  What Time Is It?

| Structures | Vocabulary | | Phonics |
|---|---|---|---|
| • What time is it? | ten | thirty | Long Vowels |
|   It's one o'clock. | eleven | forty | ee, ea, ey |
|   It's twelve fifty. | twelve | fifty | |
| • We're late. Let's go. | fifteen | late | |
| | twenty | one ~ nine | |

## Unit 4  Let's Play Badminton

| Structures | Vocabulary | | Phonics |
|---|---|---|---|
| • Let's play soccer. | play soccer | ride a bike | Review: Long Vowels |
|   Sounds good. | play basketball | make a snowman | ai, ay, ee, ea, ey |
|   Sorry, I can't. I'm busy. | play baseball | make a cake | |
| • Can you ride a bike? | play badminton | busy | |
|   Yes, I can. | fly a kite | | |

**Review 2**

# Unit 5  Is This Your Watch?

| Structures | Vocabulary | | Phonics |
|---|---|---|---|
| • Is this/that your cap? | cap | hairpin | Long Vowels |
| Yes, it is. / No, it isn't. | towel | camera | ie, igh |
| • My hairpin is green. | belt | backpack | |
| • My backpack is big/small. | watch | umbrella | |

# Unit 6  It's On the Table

| Structures | Vocabulary | | Phonics |
|---|---|---|---|
| • Where is my hat? | on the bed | hat | Long Vowels |
| It's on the table. | on the table | bat | oa, ow |
| • Where are my sunglasses? | on the desk | glove | |
| They're in the bag. | under the table | shorts | |
| • It's not here. | under the chair | scissors | |
| • I don't know. | in the box | crayons | |
| | in the bag | sunglasses | |

**Review 3**

# Unit 7  I Want a Hairpin

| Structures | Vocabulary | | Phonics |
|---|---|---|---|
| • What do you want? | a scarf | a ring | Long Vowels |
| I/We want a scarf. | a kite | mittens | ue, ui |
| • Do you want a comic book? | a puzzle | socks | |
| Yes, I do. / No, I don't. | a jump rope | shoes | |
| • Here you are. | a comic book | | |

# Unit 8  Do You Want Some Soup?

| Structures | Vocabulary | | Phonics |
|---|---|---|---|
| • Do you want some soup? | soup | apple pie | Review: Long Vowels |
| Yes, please. / No, thanks. I'm full. | water | ice cream | ie, igh, oa, ow, ue, ui |
| • Help yourself. | yogurt | cookies | |
| • It's delicious. | cheesecake | strawberries | |

**Review 4**

**11** Read and choose.
다음을 읽고 알맞은 그림을 고르세요.

Let's fly a kite.

ⓐ

ⓑ

ⓒ

ⓓ

**[12-13]** Look and choose.
그림을 보고 알맞은 것을 고르세요.

**12**

ⓐ It's seven o'clock.
ⓑ It's eight ten.
ⓒ It's two forty.
ⓓ It's eleven thirty.

**13**

ⓐ Good morning.
ⓑ Good afternoon.
ⓒ Good evening.
ⓓ Good night.

**[14-15]** Unscramble and write.
단어를 바르게 배열하여 문장을 쓰세요.

**14**
( please / sit / Don't / here, / . )

_____

**15**
( ride / Let's / a / bike / . )

_____

**16** Read and match.
알맞은 문장이 되도록 선으로 연결하세요.

(1) Good •            • talk.

(2) Don't •           • morning.

(3) It's •            • one o'clock.

**[17-18]** Read and choose.
대화를 읽고 빈칸에 알맞은 것을 고르세요.

**17**
A: Good afternoon.
B: _____

ⓐ How are you?
ⓑ What's your name?
ⓒ What time is it?
ⓓ Are you tired?

**18**
A: Let's play soccer.
B: _____ I'm busy.

ⓐ Okay.        ⓑ Sounds good.
ⓒ Sorry, I can't.   ⓓ Yes, I can.

**[19-20]** Look and write.
그림을 보고 대화의 빈칸에 알맞은 말을 쓰세요.

**19**

A: Don't _____ , _____ .
B: Oh, I'm _____ .

**20**

A: What time is _____ ?
B: It's _____ .

# Midterm TEST 3A

Institute _____

Name _____

Score _____ /100

## [1-2] Listen and choose.
다음을 듣고 알맞은 그림을 고르세요.

**1**

ⓐ    ⓑ

ⓒ   ⓓ

**2**

ⓐ 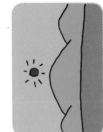   ⓑ

ⓒ   ⓓ

## 3 Listen and choose.
다음을 듣고 그림에 알맞은 것을 고르세요.

ⓐ   ⓑ

ⓒ   ⓓ

## [4-5] Listen and mark O or X.
다음을 듣고 그림과 일치하면 ○ 표, 일치하지 않으면 X 표를 하세요.

**4**   (   )

**5**  (   )

## [6-7] Listen and choose.
다음을 듣고 그림에 알맞은 응답을 고르세요.

**6**

ⓐ   ⓑ   ⓒ   ⓓ

**7**

ⓐ   ⓑ    ⓒ   ⓓ

## 8 Listen and choose.
대화를 듣고 알맞은 그림을 고르세요.

ⓐ    ⓑ

ⓒ    ⓓ

## [9-10] Listen and choose.
다음을 듣고 알맞은 응답을 고르세요.

**9** ⓐ I'm Jake.   ⓑ I'm good.

ⓒ It's snowing.   ⓓ It's five.

**10** ⓐ Not bad.   ⓑ I'm late.

ⓒ Sounds good.   ⓓ That's okay.

**11 Read and choose.**
다음을 읽고 알맞은 그림을 고르세요.

My belt is green.

ⓐ

ⓑ

ⓒ

ⓓ

**[12-13] Look and choose.**
그림을 보고 알맞은 것을 고르세요.

**12**

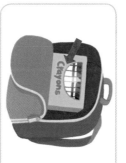

ⓐ I want a puzzle.
ⓑ I want a jump rope.
ⓒ I want mittens.
ⓓ I want socks.

**13**

ⓐ It's on the bed.
ⓑ It's on the box.
ⓒ They're in the bag.
ⓓ They're under the chair.

**[14-15] Unscramble and write.**
단어를 바르게 배열하여 문장을 쓰세요.

**14**

( Where / my / is / glove / ? )

_____

**15**

( some / Do / soup / want / you / ? )

_____

**16 Read and choose.**
빈칸에 공통으로 들어갈 알맞은 단어를 고르세요.

• I _____ a hat.
• I _____ some apple pie.

ⓐ play    ⓑ help    ⓒ want    ⓓ fly

**[17-18] Read and choose.**
대화를 읽고 빈칸에 알맞은 것을 고르세요.

**17**

A: _____
B: Yes, please.

ⓐ What do you want?
ⓑ Where is my camera?
ⓒ Is this your hairpin?
ⓓ Do you want some water?

**18**

A: Is that your backpack?
B: _____ My backpack is big.

ⓐ Yes, it is.
ⓑ No, it isn't.
ⓒ Sorry, I can't.
ⓓ It's my backpack.

**[19-20] Look and write.**
그림을 보고 대화의 빈칸에 알맞은 말을 쓰세요.

**19**

A: Where is my _____ ?
B: It's _____ the _____ .

**20**

A: Do you want a _____ ?
B: No, _____ .

# Final TEST 3A

Institute

Name

Score            /100

## [1-2] Listen and choose.
다음을 듣고 알맞은 그림을 고르세요.

**1**
ⓐ   ⓑ

ⓒ   ⓓ

**2**
ⓐ   ⓑ

ⓒ   ⓓ

## 3 Listen and choose.
다음을 듣고 그림에 알맞은 것을 고르세요.

ⓐ          ⓑ

ⓒ          ⓓ

## [4-5] Listen and mark O or X.
다음을 듣고 그림과 일치하면 O 표, 일치하지 않으면 X 표를 하세요.

**4**
 (    )   (    )

**5**
(    )

## [6-7] Listen and choose.
다음을 듣고 그림에 알맞은 응답을 고르세요.

**6**
ⓐ          ⓑ

ⓒ          ⓓ

**7**
ⓐ          ⓑ

ⓒ          ⓓ

## 8 Listen and choose.
대화를 듣고 알맞은 그림을 고르세요.

ⓐ   ⓑ

ⓒ          ⓓ

## [9-10] Listen and choose.
다음을 듣고 알맞은 응답을 고르세요.

**9**  ⓐ Yes, I am.        ⓑ Here you are.
     ⓒ No, it isn't.     ⓓ No, thanks.

**10** ⓐ Yes, please.      ⓑ Yes, it is.
     ⓒ No, I can't.      ⓓ No, I don't.

# Let's Go · 3A

Unit 1 p. 5

Unit 4 p. 31

Unit 6 p. 48

Unit 7 p. 58

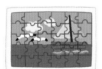  

# 2nd Edition

# LET'S GO

## to the English World

# 3A

# Word Book
# & Workbook

CHUNJAE EDUCATION, INC.

# Word Book

# How Are You?

**A** Listen and repeat. 01 02

| | | |
|---|---|---|
| | **morning** <br> 아침 | **Good** morning. <br> 안녕. (아침 인사) |
| | **afternoon** <br> 오후 | **Good** afternoon. <br> 안녕. (오후 인사) |
| | **evening** <br> 저녁 | **Good** evening. <br> 안녕. (저녁 인사) |
| | **night** <br> 밤 | **Good** night. <br> 안녕. (밤 인사) / 잘 자. |
| | **great** <br> (기분이) 아주 좋은 | **I'm** great. <br> 기분이 아주 좋아. |
| | **fine** <br> (기분이) 좋은 | **I'm** fine. <br> 기분이 좋아. |
| | **not bad** <br> (기분이) 나쁘지 않은 | Not bad. <br> 기분이 나쁘지 않아. |
| | **not so good** <br> (기분이) 별로 안좋은 | Not so good. <br> 기분이 별로 안좋아. |

B **Read, write, and say.**

**1  morning**
아침

**2  afternoon**
오후

**3  evening**
저녁

**4  night**
밤

**5  great**
(기분이) 아주 좋은

**6  fine**
(기분이) 좋은

**7  not bad**
(기분이) 나쁘지 않은

**8  not so good**
(기분이) 별로 안 좋은

**Learn More**

**how**  어떤 상태로    How **are you?** 기분이 어때?

Ⓐ **Listen and repeat.**

**talk**
말하다

**Don't** talk.
말하지 마.

**push**
밀다

**Don't** push.
밀지 마.

**enter**
들어가다

**Don't** enter.
들어가지 마.

**run**
뛰다, 달리다

**Don't** run.
뛰지 마.

**touch**
만지다

**Don't** touch, **please.**
만지지 마세요.

**take pictures**
사진을 찍다

**Don't** take pictures, **please.**
사진을 찍지 마세요.

**sit here**
여기에 앉다

**Don't** sit here, **please.**
여기에 앉지 마세요.

**eat here**
여기에서 먹다

**Don't** eat here, **please.**
여기에서 먹지 마세요.

**Read, write, and say.**

**1 talk**
말하다

**2 push**
밀다

**3 enter**
들어가다

**4 run**
뛰다, 달리다

**5 touch**
만지다

**6 take pictures**
사진을 찍다

**7 sit here**
여기에 앉다

**8 eat here**
여기에서 먹다

**Learn More**

| | |
|---|---|
| **sorry** 미안한 | I'm sorry. 미안해. |
| **okay** 괜찮은 | That's okay. 괜찮아. |

# What Time Is It?

## Ⓐ Listen and repeat. 🎧27 🎧28

| | | |
|---|---|---|
| **10** | ten 10 | It's ten o'clock. 10시야. |
| **11** | eleven 11 | It's eleven o'clock. 11시야. |
| **12** | twelve 12 | It's twelve o'clock. 12시야. |
| **15** | fifteen 15 | It's four fifteen. 4시 15분이야. |
| **20** | twenty 20 | It's five twenty. 5시 20분이야. |
| **30** | thirty 30 | It's six thirty. 6시 30분이야. |
| **40** | forty 40 | It's seven forty. 7시 40분이야. |
| **50** | fifty 50 | It's eight fifty. 8시 50분이야. |
| | late 늦은 | I'm late. 나는 늦었어. |

## B Read, write, and say.

☐Read  ☐Write  ☐Say

**1 ten**
10

**2 eleven**
11

**3 twelve**
12

**4 fifteen**
15

**5 twenty**
20

**6 thirty**
30

**7 forty**
40

**8 fifty**
50

**9 late**
늦은

### Learn More

| | |
|---|---|
| **what time** 몇 시 | What time **is it?** 몇 시니? |
| **o'clock** ~시 (정각) | **It's one** o'clock. 1시야. |

## Ⓐ Listen and repeat.

**play soccer**
축구를 하다

**Can you play soccer?**
너는 축구를 할 수 있니?

**play basketball**
농구를 하다

**Can you play basketball?**
너는 농구를 할 수 있니?

**play baseball**
야구를 하다

**Can you play baseball?**
너는 야구를 할 수 있니?

**fly a kite**
연을 날리다

**Let's fly a kite.**
연을 날리자.

**make a snowman**
눈사람을 만들다

**Let's make a snowman.**
눈사람을 만들자.

**play badminton**
배드민턴을 치다

**Let's play badminton.**
배드민턴을 치자.

**ride a bike**
자전거를 타다

**Let's ride a bike.**
자전거를 타자.

**busy**
바쁜

**I'm busy.**
나는 바빠.

## B Read, write, and say.

1  **play soccer**
축구를 하다

2  **play basketball**
농구를 하다

3  **play baseball**
야구를 하다

4  **fly a kite**
연을 날리다

5  **make a snowman**
눈사람을 만들다

6  **play badminton**
배드민턴을 치다

7  **ride a bike**
자전거를 타다

8  **busy**
바쁜

---

**Learn More**

**tired** 피곤한    I'm tired. 나는 피곤해.

**A** Listen and repeat.

**cap**
모자

**Is this your cap?**
이것은 너의 모자니?

**towel**
수건

**Is that your towel?**
저것은 너의 수건이니?

**belt**
벨트

**Where is my belt?**
내 벨트는 어디에 있니?

**watch**
손목시계

**It's my watch.**
그것은 내 손목시계야.

**hairpin**
머리핀

**My hairpin is big.**
내 머리핀은 커.

**camera**
카메라

**My camera is small.**
내 카메라는 작아.

**backpack**
배낭

**My backpack is blue.**
내 배낭은 파란색이야.

**umbrella**
우산

**My umbrella is red.**
내 우산은 빨간색이야.

## B Read, write, and say.

**1 cap**
모자

**2 towel**
수건

**3 belt**
벨트

**4 watch**
손목시계

**5 hairpin**
머리핀

**6 camera**
카메라

**7 backpack**
배낭

**8 umbrella**
우산

### Learn More

| this | 이것 | Is this your cap? 이것은 너의 모자니? |
|------|------|---------------------------------|
| that | 저것 | Is that your towel? 저것은 너의 수건이니? |
| your | 너의 | Is this your belt? 이것은 너의 벨트니? |
| my | 나의 | Where is my watch? 내 손목시계는 어디에 있니? |

# It's On the Table

## Ⓐ Listen and repeat. 🎧66 🎧67

**on the bed**
침대 위에

**It's** on the bed.
그것은 침대 위에 있어.

**on the table**
탁자 위에

**It's** on the table.
그것은 탁자 위에 있어.

**under the table**
탁자 아래에

**It's** under the table.
그것은 탁자 아래에 있어.

**in the box**
상자 안에

**It's** in the box.
그것은 상자 안에 있어.

**on the desk**
책상 위에

**It's** on the desk.
그것은 책상 위에 있어.

**under the chair**
의자 아래에

**It's** under the chair.
그것은 의자 아래에 있어.

**in the bag**
가방 안에

**It's** in the bag.
그것은 가방 안에 있어.

## B Read, write, and say.

1 **on the bed**
침대 위에

2 **on the table**
탁자 위에

3 **under the table**
탁자 아래에

4 **in the box**
상자 안에

5 **on the desk**
책상 위에

6 **under the chair**
의자 아래에

7 **in the bag**
가방 안에

**Learn More**

**where** 어디에 | Where **is my cap?** 내 모자는 어디에 있니?

# I Want a Hairpin

**a scarf**
목도리

**Do you want** a scarf**?**
너는 목도리를 원하니?

**a kite**
연

**Do you want** a kite**?**
너는 연을 원하니?

**a puzzle**
퍼즐

**I want** a puzzle**.**
나는 퍼즐을 원해.

**a jump rope**
줄넘기

**I want** a jump rope**.**
나는 줄넘기를 원해.

**a comic book**
만화책

**We want** a comic book**.**
우리는 만화책을 원해.

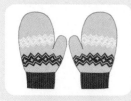

**mittens**
벙어리장갑

**We want** mittens**.**
우리는 벙어리장갑을 원해.

**socks**
양말

**They want** socks**.**
그들은 양말을 원해.

**shoes**
신발

**They want** shoes**.**
그들은 신발을 원해.

**Read, write, and say.**

☐ Read ☐ Write ☐ Say

**1  a scarf**
목도리

**2  a kite**
연

**3  a puzzle**
퍼즐

**4  a jump rope**
줄넘기

**5  a comic book**
만화책

**6  mittens**
벙어리장갑

**7  socks**
양말

**8  shoes**
신발

**Learn More**

**want** 원하다 | **What do you** want**?** 너는 무엇을 원하니?

# UNIT 8 Do You Want Some Soup?

## Ⓐ Listen and repeat. 🎧92 🎧93

**soup**
수프

**Do you want some** soup**?**
너는 수프를 좀 먹을래?

**water**
물

**Do you want some** water**?**
너는 물을 좀 마실래?

**yogurt**
요거트

**Do you want some** yogurt**?**
너는 요거트를 좀 먹을래?

**cheesecake**
치즈케이크

**I want some** cheesecake**.**
나는 치즈케이크를 좀 먹고 싶어.

**apple pie**
애플파이

**I want some** apple pie**.**
나는 애플파이를 좀 먹고 싶어.

**ice cream**
아이스크림

**I want some** ice cream**.**
나는 아이스크림을 좀 먹고 싶어.

**cookies**
쿠키 (여러 개)

**I like** cookies**.**
나는 쿠키를 좋아해.

**strawberries**
딸기 (여러 개)

**I like** strawberries**.**
나는 딸기를 좋아해.

## Ⓑ Read, write, and say.

**1 soup**
수프

**2 water**
물

**3 yogurt**
요거트

**4 cheesecake**
치즈케이크

**5 apple pie**
애플파이

**6 ice cream**
아이스크림

**7 cookies**
쿠키 (여러 개)

**8 strawberries**
딸기 (여러 개)

### Learn More

| | | |
|---|---|---|
| **some** | 조금, 약간 | Do you want some soup? 너는 수프를 좀 먹을래? |
| **full** | 배부른 | I'm full. 나는 배불러. |

# Let's GO 3A Workbook

*2nd Edition*

*to the English World*

# How Are You?

# Words

(A) **Choose and write.**

1

_____

2

_____

3

_____

4

_____

night

fine

not so good

morning

great

evening

afternoon

not bad

5

_____

6

_____

7

_____

8

_____

# Practice

**Ⓐ Look and circle.**

1. Good ( **night** / morning ).

2. Good ( **afternoon** / evening ).

3. Good ( night / **evening** ).

4. Good ( **morning** / night ).

**Ⓑ Match and write.**

How are you?

1. great

I'm _____.

2. fine

I'm _____.

3. not so good

_____

# Listen & Talk

## A Read and check.

1

A: ☐ Good afternoon.  ☐ Good evening.

B: Good afternoon.

2

A: Good night.

B: ☐ Good afternoon.  ☐ Good night.

3

A: How are you?

B: ☐ I'm great.  ☐ Not so good.

## B Choose and write.

| Not bad. How great evening morning |

1

A: Good _____.

How are you?

B: I'm _____.

2

A: Good _____.

_____ are you?

B: _____

# Write & Talk

Ⓐ **Look and write.**

1

A: Good _____.

B: _____ night, Mom.

2

A: Good _____. How are you?

B: I'm _____.

3

A: _____ afternoon. _____ are you?

B: _____ _____ good. I'm sick.

4

A: How _____ you?

B: Not _____. _____ about you?

A: I'm fine.

5

A: How are _____?

B: I'm great. How about you?

A: I'm _____. Thanks.

# Story

## A Choose and write.

| Great. Thanks. | How are you? | Not so good. |

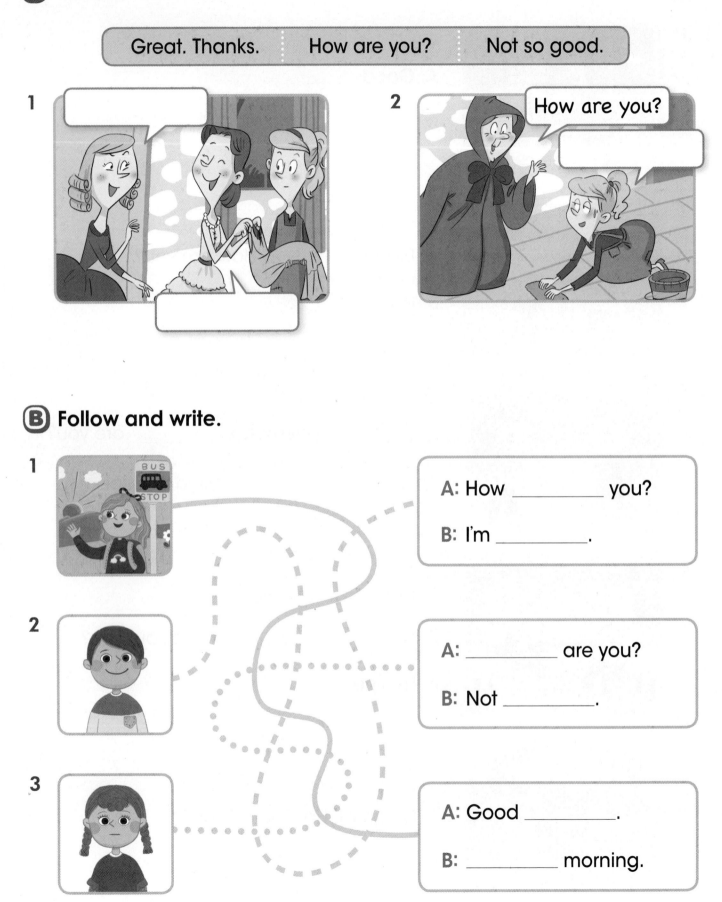

**1**

**2**
How are you?

## B Follow and write.

**1**

A: How _____ you?

B: I'm _____.

**2**

A: _____ are you?

B: Not _____.

**3**

A: Good _____.

B: _____ morning.

# Writing

## Ⓐ Make the sentence.

**1**

| morning | . | Good |

┈┈▶ _____

안녕. (아침 인사)

**2**

| night | Good | . |

┈┈▶ _____

안녕. (밤 인사) / 잘 자.

**3**

| you | How | ? | are |

┈┈▶ _____

기분이 어때?

**4**

| great | . | I'm |

┈┈▶ _____

기분이 아주 좋아.

**5**

| good | so | . | Not |

┈┈▶ _____

기분이 별로 안 좋아.

# Words

**Ⓐ Circle and write.**

1

push / run

_____

2

talk / touch

_____

3

eat here / push

_____

4

take pictures / enter

_____

5
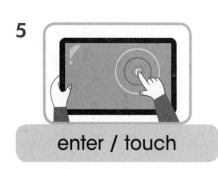
enter / touch

_____

6

sit here / eat here

_____

7

take pictures / talk

_____

8

eat here / run

_____

# Practice

## A Look and match.

1 Don't • • enter.

2 Don't • • talk.

3 Don't • • run.

4 Don't • • push.

## B Check and write.

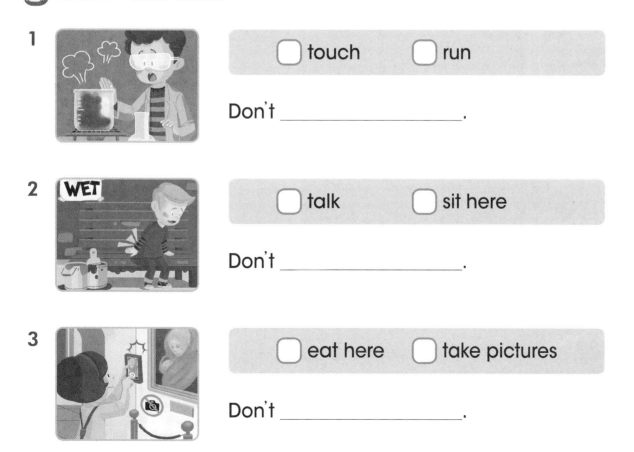

1 ☐ touch   ☐ run

Don't _____.

2 ☐ talk   ☐ sit here

Don't _____.

3 ☐ eat here   ☐ take pictures

Don't _____.

# Listen & Talk

## Ⓐ Read and number.

| 1 Don't sit here. | 2 Don't run. | 3 Don't eat here. |

## Ⓑ Choose and write.

| push   enter   talk   sorry   please   Don't |

1

A: Don't _____.

B: Okay.

2

A: Don't _____, _____.

B: Okay.

3

A: _____ _____, please.

B: Oh, I'm _____.

A: That's okay.

# Write & Talk

**A** Look and write.

1

A: _____ push.

B: Okay.

2

A: _____ _____, please.

B: Okay.

3

A: _____ _____, please.

B: Oh, I'm _____.

4

A: Don't _____ _____, please.

B: Oh, I'm sorry.

A: That's _____.

5

A: Don't _____ here, _____.

B: Oh, _____ sorry.

A: That's okay.

# Story

## Ⓐ Look and match.

1

2

3

ⓐ Don't touch, please.

ⓑ Don't sit here, please.

ⓒ Don't enter, please.

## Ⓑ Look and write.

1 A: Don't _____ _____,

　　 please.

　 B: Okay.

2 A: _____ _____, please.

　 B: Oh, I'm sorry.

3 A: Don't _____, _____.

　 B: Oh, I'm _____.

# Writing

## Ⓐ Make the sentence.

**1**

take  .  Don't  pictures

...▶ _____

사진 찍지 마.

**2**

Don't  please  .  run  ,

...▶ _____

뛰지 마세요.

**3**

enter  ,  Don't  .  please

...▶ _____

들어가지 마세요.

**4**

Don't  here  ,  eat  .  please

...▶ _____

여기에서 먹지 마세요.

**5**

I'm  Oh  ,  sorry  .

...▶ _____

오, 미안해.

# What Time Is It?

## Words

### (A) Match and write.

1

_____

2

_____

3

_____

4

_____

ten

eleven

twelve

fifteen

twenty

thirty

forty

fifty

5

_____

6

_____

7

_____

8

_____

# Practice

## A Read and circle.

**1**

It's ( eleven / twelve ) o'clock.

**2**

It's four ( twenty / thirty ).

**3**

It's nine ( forty / fifty ).

**4**

It's seven ( ten / fifteen ).

## B Connect and write.

What time is it?

**1**

08 : 20

It's

| eight | forty. |
|-------|--------|
| four | twenty. |

...▸ _____

**2**

12 : 50

It's

| seven | fifty. |
|-------|--------|
| twelve | fifteen. |

...▸ _____

**3**

06 : 10

It's

| six | ten. |
|-----|------|
| nine | thirty. |

...▸ _____

# Listen & Talk

## A Read and draw.

What time is it?

**1**

It's four o'clock.

**2**

It's eleven forty.

**3**

It's twelve thirty.

**4**

It's one fifty.

## B Choose and write.

What   ten   time   it   fifty   fifteen

**1**

A: What _____ is it?

B: It's twelve _____.

**2**

A: What time is _____?

B: It's three _____.

**3**

A: _____ time is it?

B: It's eight _____.

34

# Write & Talk

**A** Look and write.

**1**

A: _____ time is it?

B: It's six _____.

**2**

A: What time is _____?

B: It's two _____.

**3**

A: What _____ is it?

B: It's _____ _____.

**4**

A: _____ time _____ it?

B: It's eight _____.

A: Oh, _____ late.

**5**

A: What _____ is it?

B: _____ two _____.

A: We're _____. Let's go.

# Story

## A Choose and write.

| What time is it? | It's two o'clock. | It's two thirty. |

**1**

**2**

## B Match and write.

**1**

**a**

A: What _____ is it?

B: It's _____ o'clock.

**2**

**b**

A: What time is _____?

B: It's _____ thirty.

**3**

**c**

A: _____ time is it?

B: It's eight _____.

# Writing

## A Make the sentence.

1

| time | What | it | is | ? |

···▶ _____

몇 시예요?

2

| twelve | o'clock | . | It's |

···▶ _____

12시야.

3

| six | . | It's | fifty |

···▶ _____

6시 50분이야.

4

| It's | twenty | . | seven |

···▶ _____

7시 20분이야.

5

| . | We're | late |

···▶ _____

우리는 늦었어.

# Let's Play Badminton

# Words

## Ⓐ Look and check.

1

☐ play baseball
☐ play soccer

2

☐ ride a bike
☐ fly a kite

3

☐ play badminton
☐ play basketball

4

☐ make a snowman
☐ fly a kite

5

☐ play soccer
☐ play basketball

6

☐ ride a bike
☐ make a snowman

7

☐ play baseball
☐ play badminton

8

☐ sick
☐ busy

# Practice

## Ⓐ Choose and write.

| soccer   baseball   badminton   basketball |

1

Let's play _____.

2

Let's play _____.

3

Let's play _____.

4

Let's play _____.

## Ⓑ Circle and write.

1

A: Let's _____.

( ride a bike / make a snowman )

B: Sounds good.

2

A: Let's _____.

( play badminton / fly a kite )

B: Sorry, I can't.

# Listen & Talk

## Ⓐ Read, match, and check.

1  Let's play badminton.  •

ⓐ    ☐ Sounds good.
      ☐ Sorry, I can't.

2  Let's play basketball.  •

ⓑ    ☐ Sounds good.
      ☐ Sorry, I can't.

3  Let's ride a bike.  •

ⓒ    ☐ Sounds good.
      ☐ Sorry, I can't.

## Ⓑ Choose and write.

1

A: Let's _____ .

B: Sounds good.

2

A: Let's _____ .

B: _____ I like baseball.

3

A: Let's _____ .

B: _____ I'm tired.

---

make a snowman    Sorry, I can't.    Sounds good.    fly a kite    play baseball

# Write & Talk

## Ⓐ Look and write.

**1**

A: Let's play _____.

B: Sounds _____.

**2**

A: Let's _____ soccer.

B: Sorry, I _____. I'm tired.

**3**

A: Let's _____ a _____.

B: _____ good.

**4**

A: _____ _____ basketball.

B: Sounds good. I like _____.

**5**

A: Let's _____ a _____.

B: _____, I can't. _____ busy.

# Story

## Ⓐ Read and match.

**1**

**2**

**3**

ⓐ
A: Let's ride a bike.
B: Sorry, I can't. I'm busy.

ⓑ
A: Let's make a cake.
B: Sounds good.

ⓒ
A: Let's play badminton.
B: Sorry, I can't. I'm tired.

## Ⓑ Look and write.

**1**

A: Can you _____ a _____?

B: Yes, I can.

A: _____ ride a bike.

B: Sounds _____.

**2**

A: It's snowing.

Let's _____ a snowman.

B: _____, I _____. I'm tired.

A: That's okay.

# Writing

## Ⓐ Make the sentence.

1

Let's   .   basketball   play

···▶ _____

농구를 하자.

2

bike   a   Let's   .   ride

···▶ _____

자전거를 타자.

3

a   Let's   .   kite   fly

···▶ _____

연을 날리자.

4

good   .   Sounds

···▶ _____

좋아.

5

I   ,   Sorry   can't   .

···▶ _____

미안하지만 안 돼.

# Is This Your Watch?

# Words

**A** Complete the puzzle.

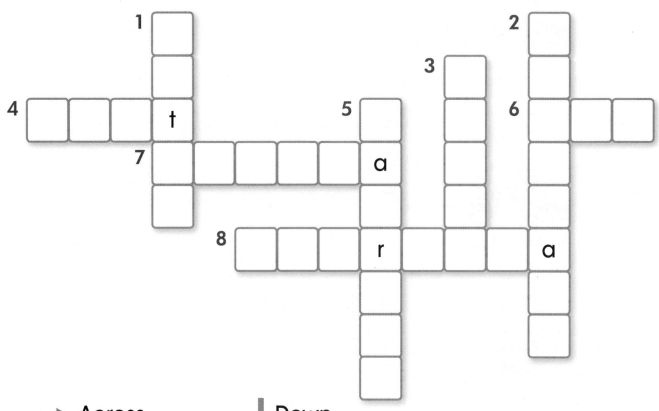

1 │ 2 │ 3 │ 4 t │ 5 a │ 6 │ 7 r │ 8 a

→ Across

4

6

7

8

↓ Down

1

2

3

5

cap

towel

watch

belt

hairpin

backpack

camera

umbrella

# Practice

**A** Circle and mark O or X.

1    2    3    4

1  A: Is this your ( towel / watch )?        B: Yes, it is.

2  A: Is this your ( camera / cap )?        B: No, it isn't.

3  A: Is this your ( hairpin / umbrella )?  B: No, it isn't.

4  A: Is this your ( backpack / belt )?     B: Yes, it is.


**B** Choose, write, and circle.

> towel   camera   umbrella

1

A: Is this your _____?

B: ( Yes, it is. / No, it isn't. )

2

A: Is this your _____?

B: ( Yes, it is. / No, it isn't. )

3

A: Is this your _____?

B: ( Yes, it is. / No, it isn't. )
   My umbrella is green.

# Listen & Talk

## Ⓐ Read and check.

**1**

A: ☐ Is this your watch?

☐ Is this your backpack?

B: Yes, it is.

**2**

A: ☐ Is that your towel?

☐ Is that your camera?

B: No, it isn't.

**3**

A: Is this your cap?

B: ☐ Yes, it is.

☐ No, it isn't. My cap is red.

## Ⓑ Choose and write.

| it   this   belt   big   hairpin   that |

**1**

A: Is _____ your _____?

B: Yes, _____ is.

**2**

A: Is _____ your _____?

B: No, it isn't. My hairpin is _____.

# Write & Talk

**Ⓐ Look and write.**

**1**

A: Is _____ your _____?

B: _____, it is.

**2**

A: Is _____ your towel?

B: _____, it isn't. My towel is _____.

**3**

A: Is this _____ hairpin?

B: Yes, it _____. It's my _____.

**4**

A: Is this your _____?

B: No, it _____.

_____ backpack is _____.

**5**

A: Where is my _____?

B: Is _____ your camera?

A: Yes, _____ is. Thank you.

# Story

## Ⓐ Circle, choose, and write.

**1**

A: Is ( this / that ) your _____?

B: Yes, it is.

**2**

A: Is ( this / that ) your _____?

B: No, it isn't. My backpack is yellow.

**3**

A: ( This / That ) is my _____.

B: It's nice.

## Ⓑ Look and write.

**1**

A: Is that your _____?

B: Yes, _____ _____.

**2**

A: Is _____ your belt?

B: No, _____ _____.

My belt is _____.

# Writing

## Ⓐ Make the sentence.

**1**

| this | belt | Is | your | ? |

...▸ _____

이것은 네 벨트니?

**2**

| your | Is | ? | that | backpack |

...▸ _____

저것은 네 배낭이니?

**3**

| my | This | watch | . | is |

...▸ _____

이것은 내 손목시계야.

**4**

| big | . | My | is | towel |

...▸ _____

내 수건은 커.

**5**

| is | red | My | . | hairpin |

yellow    red

...▸ _____

내 머리핀은 빨간색이야.

# It's On the Table

# Words

Ⓐ Circle and write.

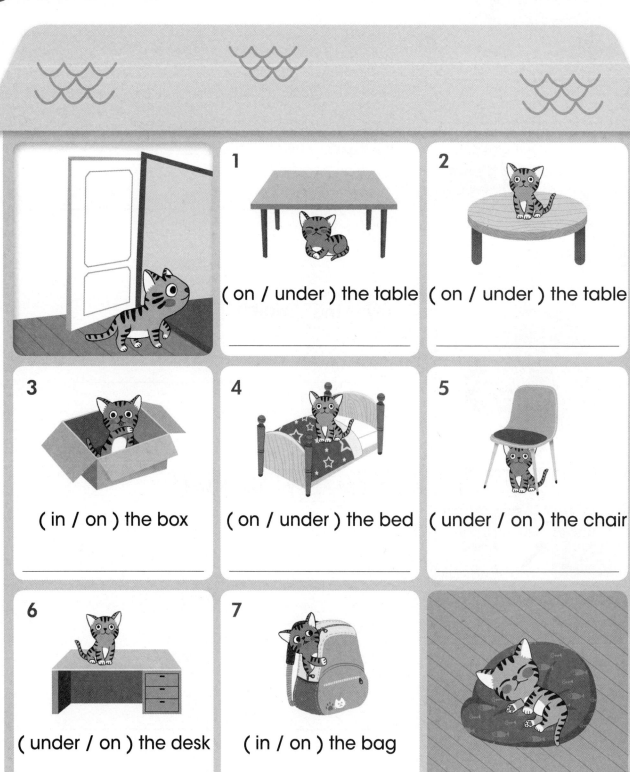

**1** ( on / under ) the table

**2** ( on / under ) the table

**3** ( in / on ) the box

**4** ( on / under ) the bed

**5** ( under / on ) the chair

**6** ( under / on ) the desk

**7** ( in / on ) the bag

# Practice

## (A) Look and number.

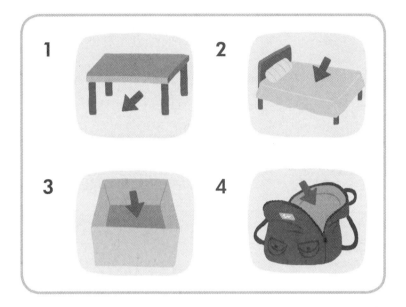

1
2
3
4

◯ It's in the box.

◯ It's on the bed.

◯ It's in the bag.

◯ It's under the table.

## (B) Circle, check, and write.

1

A: Where is my ( T-shirt / cap )?

B: It's _____.

☐ on the desk

☐ under the desk

2

A: Where is my ( bat / ball )?

B: It's _____.

☐ on the table

☐ under the chair

# Listen & Talk

## A Read and match.

1 Where are my scissors?

It's under the table.

2 Where is my glove?

It's on the chair.

3 Where is my watch?

They're in the bag.

## B Match, choose, and write.

| in  shorts  under  cap  book  on |

1

ⓐ
A: Where is my _____?

B: It's _____ the box.

2

ⓑ
A: Where is my _____?

B: It's _____ the bed.

3

ⓒ
A: Where are my _____?

B: They're _____ the desk.

# Write & Talk

**Ⓐ Look and write.**

**1**
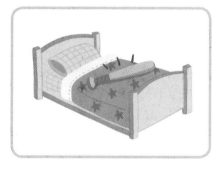

A: Where is my _____?

B: It's _____ the bed.

**2**

A: Where _____ my sunglasses?

B: They're _____ the table.

**3**

A: _____ are my crayons?

B: They're _____ the _____.

A: Thank you.

**4**

A: Where is my _____?

B: I don't know.

C: It's _____ the _____.

**5**

A: Where is my _____?

B: It's _____ the _____.

A: No, it's _____ here.

# Story

## A Match and write.

1

   **a**
   **A:** Where are my bags?
   **B:** They're _____ the tree.

2

   **b**
   **A:** Where is my belt?
   **B:** It's _____ the bed.

3

   **c**
   **A:** Where is my hat?
   **B:** It's _____ the box.

## B Look and write.

1  **A:** Where is my cap?
   **B:** It's _____ the _____.

2  **A:** Where _____ my _____?
   **B:** It's _____ the box.

3  **A:** Where _____ my _____?
   **B:** They're _____ the table.

# Writing

## Ⓐ Make the sentence.

**1**

| Where | watch | my | is | ? |

⋯▸ _____

내 손목시계는 어디에 있니?

**2**

| on | chair | . | It's | the |

⋯▸ _____

그것은 의자 위에 있어.

**3**

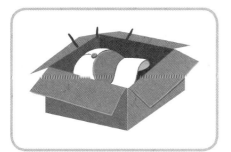

| the | . | box | in | It's |

⋯▸ _____

그것은 상자 안에 있어.

**4**

| books | my | Where | ? | are |

⋯▸ _____

내 책들은 어디에 있니?

**5**

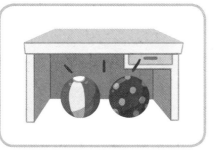

| desk | the | They're | . | under |

⋯▸ _____

그것들은 책상 아래에 있어.

# I Want a Hairpin

## Words

**A** Follow, choose, and write.

1 _____
2 _____
3 _____
4 _____

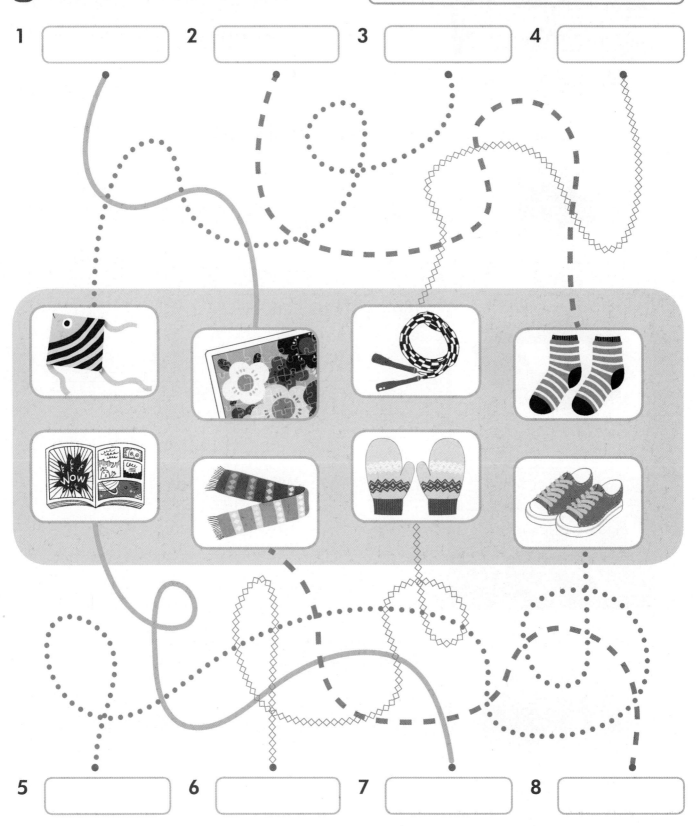

5 _____
6 _____
7 _____
8 _____

# Practice

## A Look and match.

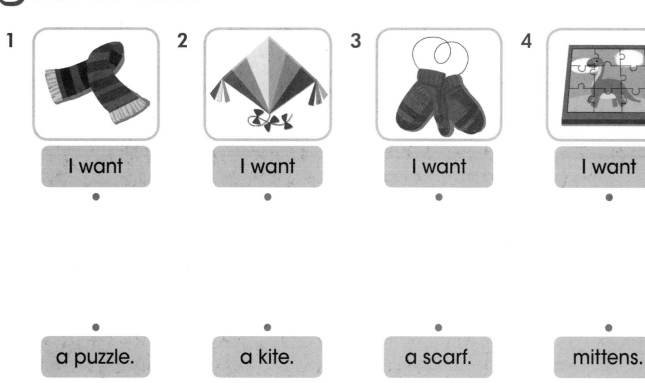

1 I want
2 I want
3 I want
4 I want

a puzzle.    a kite.    a scarf.    mittens.

## B Circle and write.

What do you want?

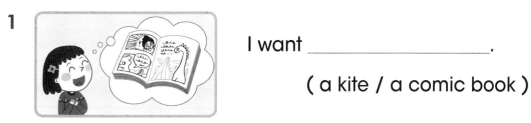

1 I want _____.
( a kite / a comic book )

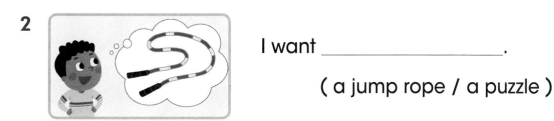

2 I want _____.
( a jump rope / a puzzle )

3 I want _____.
( socks / shoes )

# Listen & Talk

## (A) Read and write the letter.

1
A: What do you want?
B: I want a comic book. ⭕

2
A: What do you want?
B: We want a puzzle. ⭕

3
A: Do you want a scarf?
B: No, I don't. I want mittens. ⭕

## (B) Choose and write.

kite    Do    shoes    jump rope    ball    want

1
A: What do you want?
B: I want _____.

2
A: What do you _____?
B: We want a _____.

3
A: _____ you want a _____?
B: No, I don't.
I want a _____.

# Write & Talk

## Ⓐ Look and write.

**1**

A: What do you _____?

B: I want a _____.

**2**

A: What do you want?

B: _____ want a _____.

**3**

A: Do you want a _____?

B: Yes, I _____.

A: Here _____ are.

**4**

A: Do you want a hat?

B: _____, I don't.

I _____ a _____.

**5**

A: Do you want _____?

B: No, I don't.

A: _____ do you want?

B: I want _____.

# Story

## A Read and circle.

1

A: What do you want?

B: I want ( a jump rope / a ball ).

2

A: Do you want a kite?

B: ( Yes, I do. / No, I don't. )

3

A: What do you want?

B: I want ( socks / mittens ).

## B Read and write.

1  A: What do you want?          B: I want _____.

2  A: What do you want?          B: I want _____.

3  A: Do you want _____?   B: No, I don't. I want _____.

# Writing

## Ⓐ Make the sentence.

**1**

What | you | do | want | ?

...▶ _____

너는 무엇을 원하니?

**2**

want | . | I | shoes

...▶ _____

나는 신발을 원해.

**3**

puzzle | We | a | . | want

...▶ _____

우리는 퍼즐을 원해.

**4**

They | . | comic book | want | a

...▶ _____

그들은 만화책을 원해.

**5**

you | ? | want | Do | mittens

...▶ _____

너는 벙어리장갑을 원하니?

# Do You Want Some Soup?

# Words

(A) **Choose and write.**

1

_____

2

_____

3

_____

4
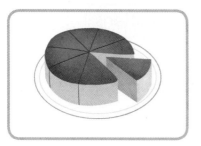

_____

yogurt

water

cheesecake

ice cream

cookies

apple pie

strawberries

soup

5

_____

6

_____

7

_____

8

_____

# Practice

## A Circle and mark O or X.

| 1 | 2 | 3 | 4 |
|---|---|---|---|
|  |  | 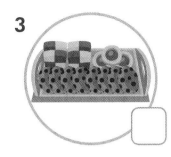 | 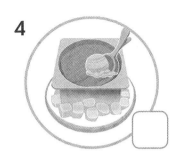 |

1  A: Do you want some ( yogurt / apple pie )?    B: Yes, please.

2  A: Do you want some ( soup / strawberries )?    B: No, thanks.

3  A: Do you want some ( apple pie / cookies )?    B: No, thanks.

4  A: Do you want some ( ice cream / cheesecake )?    B: Yes, please.

## B Choose, write, and check.

cheesecake    strawberries    water

1

A: Do you want some _____?

B: ☐ Yes, please.
   ☐ No, thanks.

2

A: Do you want some _____?

B: ☐ Yes, please.
   ☐ No, thanks.

3

A: Do you want some _____?

B: ☐ Yes, please.
   ☐ No, thanks.

# Listen & Talk

## Ⓐ Read, match, and choose.

1

> A: Do you want some cheesecake?
>
> B: Yes, please.

2

> A: Do you want some yogurt?
>
> B: No, thanks.

3

> A: Do you want some cookies?
>
> B: No, thanks.

| soup | ice cream | apple pie |
| --- | --- | --- |
| Yes, please. | | No, thanks. |

## Ⓑ Choose and write.

1

A: Do you want some _____?

B: _____

2

A: Do you want some _____?

B: _____

3

A: Do you want some _____?

B: _____ I'm full.

64

# Write & Talk

**Ⓐ Look and write.**

**1**

A: Do you want some _____?

B: Yes, _____.

**2**

A: Do you want some _____?

B: No, _____. I'm full.

**3**

A: Do you want _____ yogurt?

B: Yes, please. I like _____.

**4**

A: Do you _____ some _____?

B: Yes, please.

A: _____ yourself.

**5**

A: _____ you want some cheesecake?

B: No, thanks.

A: _____ do you want?

B: I want some _____.

# Story

**A** Choose and write.

I want some carrot soup.
Yes, please.
Do you want some cheesecake?

What do you want?

1 _____

2 _____

3 _____

**B** Read and write.

1 A: Do you want some _____? B: Yes, please.

2 A: Do you want some _____? B: No, thanks.

3 A: Do you want some _____? B: _____

4 A: Do you want some _____? B: _____

# Writing

## Ⓐ Make the sentence.

**1**

| want | Do | water | you | some | ? |

···▸ _____

너는 물을 좀 마실래?

**2**

| Do | apple pie | you | some | ? | want |

···▸ _____

너는 애플파이를 좀 먹을래?

**3**

| I | yogurt | some | . | want |

···▸ _____

나는 요거트를 좀 원해.

**4**

| some | want | cookies | . | We |

···▸ _____

우리는 쿠키를 좀 원해.

**5**

| you | ? | What | want | do |

···▸ _____

너는 무엇을 원하니?